THE MOUNTFIELD LINE SINCE 2000

CHRIS LIVINGS

First published 2026

Amberley Publishing
The Hill, Stroud
Gloucestershire, GL5 4EP

www.amberley-books.com

Copyright © Chris Livings, 2026

The right of Chris Livings to be identified as the Author of this work has been asserted in accordance with the Copyrights, Designs and Patents Act 1988.

ISBN 978 1 3981 3024 1 (print)
ISBN 978 1 3981 3025 8 (ebook)

All rights reserved. No part of this book may be reprinted or reproduced or utilised in any form or by any electronic, mechanical or other means, now known or hereafter invented, including photocopying and recording, or in any information storage or retrieval system, without the permission in writing from the Publishers.

British Library Cataloguing in Publication Data.
A catalogue record for this book is available from the British Library.

Typesetting by SJmagic DESIGN SERVICES, India.
Printed in the UK.

Appointed GPSR EU Representative:
Easy Access System Europe Oü, 16879218
Address: Mustamäe tee 50, 10621, Tallinn, Estonia
Contact Details: gpsr.requests@easproject.com, +358 40 500 3575

Introduction and History

Known by some as the gypsum mine tramway or just plain mineral line, the building of a railway in Mountfield village 3 miles north of Battle in East Sussex commenced in 1876, thereby reaching, in 2026, 150 years of almost continuous operation. The railway opened fully a year later and was built mainly to provide a link in the transportation of product from the Mountfield gypsum mine to the nearby Hastings to Charing Cross line of the then South Eastern Railway.

This book sets out for the main part to illustrate the modern era of whole train operations, depicting the locomotives, with some detail, that travelled on the Mountfield line, and the Hastings line it feeds into.

The rural aspect of the line has lost very little of its appeal over the years, and is much the same today as described in a 1936 issue of the *Sussex County Magazine*.

The mine – for a mine it is, in every sense of the word – is reached by a railway track which winds its way for around a mile through a woodland valley, alongside a rippling stream. In the springtime, the banks on either side are carpeted with primroses and violets, and as the loco puffs its way along, rabbits run, scuttling in all directions. The journey's end is unexpected and surprising. Unexpected, because little or no sign of the works can be seen until immediately before they are reached, and surprising because of their extensive nature. The buildings stand in a hollow so crowded round with thickly wooded slopes that it is impossible to obtain a view of them as a whole. Wildflowers grow up to the very doors and even around the buildings, as if nature were determined not to concede to industry an inch more than is necessary.

Gypsum is a very useful mineral and is a key ingredient in all sorts of well-known products. Raw gypsum would have been extracted from the Mountfield mine and sent away by train as an essential part in, amongst other things, the making of glass, paint products, school chalk and fertilizers.

Today the site is a plasterboard plant. Owing to depleted stocks at Mountfield, gypsum was until 1993 transported by a 4-mile conveyor from another mine in Brightling which opened in 1963, with further material imported in through the railway system.

The mine was established in 1872 as the Sub-Wealden Borehole and was intended by its leading promoters as a purely scientific exercise. It may be, though, that some of the lengthy list of financial supporters hoped coal would be found. The borings commenced in August 1872 and again in February 1875. On both occasions accidents happened due to the drilling rods and work was abandoned.

No coal was found but at various depths thick seams of gypsum were revealed. Gypsum having been discovered, a shaft was sunk within around 60 yards of the experimental borings on land belonging to Mr C. A. Egerton.

The Sub-Wealden Gypsum Company Limited was formed in May 1876. The shaft which had reached the upper seam of gypsum was 4 miles from the nearest railway station at Robertsbridge and 1 mile from the nearest road.

The works were commenced under great difficulties as no building materials or machinery of any importance or weight could be brought to the shaft and had to be carted over hilly country, in part over field roads. The cost of carriage in winter was as high as £1 per ton. Consequently, nothing really practical could be done until railway sidings had been arranged, put in, and a railway had been constructed to connect the siding with the shaft over a mile away. There was some considerable delay. However, any troubles were overcome and in 1876 some gypsum was sent away.

The Mountfield line and sidings situated between Mountfield tunnel, which is immediately north of the sidings, and Eatenden Lane level crossing just to the south, on the Robertsbridge to Battle section of main line, had taken over fourteen months to complete, the work having started on 1 September 1876. The cost of building the line came to £322. The sidings were lengthened in 1937 and again in 1965.

The first steam locomotive arrived on 11 November 1877, built by The Yorkshire Engine Company, Sheffield, in 1871 and named *Charles Augustus* after the earlier mentioned Mr C. A. Egerton, the local squire, upon whose land the gypsum mine was built. No. 165 was a saddle tank with a 0-4-0-wheel arrangement, and had come from Greystone Lime Company, Betchworth, Surrey. In 1904 it left to go to the Brush Electrical Engineering Company Ltd. It would appear that this engine was the only one in use for the next twenty-three years, even though the railway had been extended to its full length of 1.5 miles in 1877. A Mr James Wilks is recorded as driving the first steam locomotive at Mountfield; he eventually switched trades, taking over the local bakery.

In 1899 an 0-4-0 saddle tank, *Mountfield*, 1575, was purchased from loco builders W. G. Bagnall Ltd, Stafford. In 1949 it was sold to British Plasterboard Nottinghamshire.

In 1906 a further engine was required, named *Sirapite* after a new type of plaster the company had evolved. Built by Aveling and Porter, a four-wheeled, geared transmission well tank, it gave some trouble due to a tendency to leave the track. 6158 was eventually sold to Richard Garrett Works Ltd at Leiston, Surrey, in November 1929. The locomotive still exists, at The Long Shop Museum, Leiston, in Suffolk.

Steam traction reigned on the line for ninety years. Andrew Barclay 0-6-0 saddle tank 2241 *Kemp* was one of six locomotives the company owned. (Mountfield Village Historic Society)

The need for additional engine power increased and an 0-4-0 saddle tank, 2369 *Sirapite No. 2*, was purchased from W. G. Bagnall in 1928. After nearly forty years of service the locomotive was scrapped on site.

Another 0-4-0 was obtained from the Sentinel Works in 1948. It was an unnamed four-wheeled locomotive with geared transmission and a vertical boiler, and numbered 9382. This too was scrapped on site in September 1967.

The need for a sixth engine was decided upon by the company to dispense with the need to hire locomotives from the Southern Region. Delivered in 1948 from locomotive builder Andrew Barclay in Kilmarnock, it was a 0-6-0 saddle tank, 2241 and named *Kemp* after William Joel Kemp, managing director of the gypsum mine company.

The scrapping of this and other steam locomotives on site by Thomas Ward Ltd in September 1967 must have made a very sad sight for loco crews.

The rolling stock of the company is vague, but it was reported that in 1950 it comprised of a quantity of eight and ten box vans for the internal movement of gypsum and also between the various departments.

The steam era on the internal works system was well and truly over when the company purchased twin four-wheeled diesel hydraulic locomotives, works numbers 183V and 184V, built by Thomas Hill Ltd at their Kilnhurst site. New to Mountfield on 14 June and 8 August, none of the locomotives were named, but they did carry the legend British Gypsum No. 1 or 2 respectfully on their lime green cab sides.

There is no record of the line ever being used regularly to carry passengers. Nevertheless, on Saturday 7 June 1934 the *Hastings and St Leonards Observer* reported, 'Thirty members of the

Thomas Hill Vanguard No. 2 was one of two locomotives that, with sister engine No. 1, took the line into the modern age. (Adrian Nicholls)

Battle chamber of commerce visited the Mountfield Gypsum Mines on Wednesday afternoon and spent an enjoyable and instructive time in inspecting the extensive works. The party, headed by Mr. A.H. Povey (chairman) were met by messrs H. and L. Kemp, R. Collins and T. Ballard. They were taken on the private railway, the track of which is about a mile long, and were shown over the works where the famous Sirapite plaster and plaster of Paris are made.' Quite what they travelled in is unclear.

From the start of railway operations in 1876 until the internal works system came to an end in 1993, the gypsum line's primary job was quite simply to haul wagons from the mine to the exchange sidings adjacent to the main line, for collection to various locations by main-line locomotives.

The type of locomotive and stock used on these workings was restricted due to narrow clearances through the Hastings line tunnels, which included Mountfield. Not a lot is known about the early years of freight workings in the area; however, Southern Railway's 0-6-0 Q1 Class locomotives built in 1942 were recorded as operating on the line.

The working timetable for freight in 1956 showed, on an ordinary weekday, five down and seven up trains starting from or terminating at Tonbridge West Yard. Coal and general freight were conveyed southwards, however most of the up traffic was from the gypsum mine – around this period, approx. 375,500 tons of lump gypsum were transported in open wagons mainly to works in north Kent. Approx. 33,800 tons of plaster in 'shocvans' were consigned by rail to various destinations. Following the disastrous North Sea flooding in January 1953 thousands of tons of gypsum were railed from Mountfield to the north Kent coastal region to counteract the effect of salt water on the land.

With the delivery commencing in 1962 of the St Leonards-based narrow-bodied diesel Class 33/2s D6586–D6597 for use on the Hastings to Tonbridge line, the few remaining steam locomotive operations over the route were either withdrawn or transferred away.

In 1975 the double-track line through Mountfield tunnel was singled. The track alterations made it possible for trains to run straight into the exchange sidings. For many years proceeding this the access into the siding had always been by a trailing connection into the up line.

Stuart S. recalls that, 'Prior to this date. Mountfield exchange sidings were still on the up side of the line south of the tunnel. In my day, 1975, the Eatenden Lane level crossing just south of the exchange sidings had been replaced by half barriers. A new ground frame building was built near the tunnel. The frame was released from Robertsbridge. Before Mountfield tunnel was single-tracked, the gypsum train was sent to Battle so the locomotive could run round its wagons and crossover to the up line and proceed to Mountfield. There the Mountfield loco could remove the empty wagons so they could proceed onto the mines complex hauled by one of British Gypsum's own locomotives. The boundary gate was then closed by the shunters or a signal cabin worker.' A memory of Mountfield operations that must have been inconvenient on a busy main line.

On arrival at Mountfield the train's locomotive would be inside Mountfield tunnel, which is on a curve. The push back was dealt with in a very novel way indeed. On the tunnel wall were three bells, the first only a few yards in, then another further along, and so forth. There was always a shunter in attendance; when the train had a passed the trailing points the shunter would ring the stop signal, then when the road was set, he would ring a setback signal and the driver would propel back into the sidings.

The main traffic flow at the time was to Northfleet cement works in Kent which had started in 1970. The train travelled up the Hastings line through Tonbridge, then took the Lee-Curve, on to the Sidcup line, through Dartford, and on to Northfleet.

Things in the exchange sidings didn't always run smoothly, as Tony. H. remembers: 'It was a quiet afternoon sometime in 1975 or it might have been 1976. I was on a late turn and probably writing out the rosters for the next week. Supervisor Harry puts his head around the office door. "We're off the road at Mountfield", one pair of wheels. I didn't have a car in those days, so the pair of us went up in his car. Sure enough, the last axle on the last 16-ton mineral wagon of loaded gypsum had derailed towards the head shunt cess, mercifully away from the main line running alongside. The permanent way inspector was there and we discussed what to do.

The official option was to chock up the wagon on a pair of loose sleepers and slew the errant wagon back on its rails. That'll take a couple of hours, once we get the Lucas gear from Tonbridge. "That train won't be getting away tonight; the driver will be out of hours."

I asked him what was the alternative; I couldn't stand the idea of delaying traffic. We can try to put it back the same way as it came off. Put a chock under the wheels and the engine can pull it over the chock, "hopefully it'll land back on the track". I ignored the word "hopefully" and decided that would be the better and cheaper option. "Of course, if it goes wrong, you'll have to take it," he warned, which I accepted. I trusted an expert.

So, we choked up the wheels while I went to advise the driver what we were going to do. When I gave him the signal from alongside the wagon, he should carefully draw forward. Bear in mind the siding is on a curve and the locomotive is twenty wagons away from where we are. I gave the signal. I heard the engine revving up and saw movement. One by one the wagon couplings took up the slack but by the time they reached our wagon, there was appreciable speed underway. The derailed wagon snatched, rode up over the choke … and turned over, depositing its load onto the up main line. I had a lot of explaining to do.'

A little under ten years later the writer Norman Johnson visited the line for the *Kent and East Sussex Railway Magazine*. This was when the Thomas Hill Vanguard diesel shunting locos were operating on the line.

'During July 1984 by kind permission of British Gypsum Ltd, I was able to visit the rail installation at Mountfield to travel the line on the footplate, and I was surprised to find a modern railway, although, regrettably it has been somewhat rationalised over the years.

I found the operational section single line throughout, exactly 1 mile long, having been reduced from an original 1.5 miles. Commencing at the western end at the lump gypsum overhead loading plant, after loading wagons in rakes of four were propelled down a ruling gradient of 1 in 40. The train stopping frequently to allow the accompanying shunter to switch catch points to the main line to enable the train to proceed.

On the return working of empty stock, the catchpoints were reset in order to derail potential run-aways; this plus continuous air braking, ensured safe propelling on the down gradient.

An up-to-date touch was a number of two-aspect colour light signals en route linked mainly to traffic signals on the internal works open road level crossing. Although one semaphore which appeared to have protected the entry to the exchange sidings since some indeterminable time in the past stood rusting.' The operations witnessed by Norman would within ten years completely change.

The sidings at the time were under British Rail ownership. The locomotive crews employed by the gypsum company were all supplied with a BR rulebook and associated publications. Even the weekly notices would be supplied. They were also given an annual rules exam by a BR inspector even though they didn't travel over the main line as such.

In the exchange sidings trains formed of up to nineteen wagons which would await a BR locomotive and then onward haulage to Northfleet. The air-braked wagons which worked through from Mountfield were top/bottom discharge HBA hoppers built by BR engineering at their Ashford works and were owned by the Blue Circle cement company.

During 1984 loads dispatched varied between thirty-eight and 133 wagons per week compared with 250 in 1955, reflecting the inevitable loss to road haulage, although it must be kept in mind that very much larger-capacity wagons were currently in use.

The Class 33/2s operated from Mountfield until electrification of the Hastings line in 1986, after which the class could no longer be used because the train loads were increased. This put the locos beyond the maximum trailing weight permitted for their use on the route.

To cope with the increased payload additional PGA wagons were brought in from Oxwellmains cement works in Scotland to bolster the fleet and the loco haulage went over to Class 47s, which could haul twenty-three or twenty-four wagons as apposed to the Class 33's/2's nineteen. However, the 47s found the gradients near Stonegate slippery on wet days because they didn't have sanding equipment and so the haulage went over to Class 56s, which could haul even greater loads. This allowed the workings to be reduced to just two days a week, this lasting till 1993 when the only rail working operating to Northfleet ceased.

Adrian N. recalls his time during the 1980s and 1990s: 'When I worked into the exchange sidings, we had very little to do with the British Gypsum staff; only the resident shunter/ground frame operator did. As traincrew we sometimes had to sit in our locomotive to await the last cut of wagons to arrive from the mine loader. Being a freight guard, I would tie onto the train and walk around it to check the numbers given to me by the shunter while a C and W examiner from Hastings would show up in a van to check the wagons and do a brake continuity test. After that I would write out a driver's slip and we would draw up to the exit signal and wait departure.

The BR shunter at Mountfield was an old guy known as "Lofty". He had been a freight guard at Tonbridge when I was there in the mid-1980s but I believe got accommodated through ill health working at Mountfield to operate the ground frame and do the TOPS paperwork. He retired when the last train ran on 19 March 1993, so after that the sidings were in effect mothballed.'

Due to the virtual exhaustion of the Mountfield mine an unusual turn of events came about as the site began importing desulphurized powder gypsum. This BR working using Class 60 locomotives began arriving from Drax power station or Southampton Docks during February 1994.

On privatisation EWS inherited the contract from BR, which in turn was taken over by GBRF in March 2003 and then Freightliner in 2024.

The Mountfield Branch Line

By the year 2000 the Class 60s had been operating over the line for five years. The class was affectionately known as 'Mountain Movers' due to its massive potential power output, and appropriately named after the highest mountain peaks in the UK. Getting away in style, 60064 *Black Tor* leaves the exchange sidings. 7.12.99.

A view from a footpath that passes between Mountfield Church and Eatenden Lane, 66073 is glimpsed in its original EWS livery. The company later became DB Schenker Ltd in 2009 and DB Cargo in 2016. 15.6.99.

GBRF locomotive 66724 is powering its train up the line. After unloading normally, it would propel the wagons down the line. The warning sign was to be observed if a locomotive was needed to lead down the line. 18.3.15.

Positioned at the unloading area near the top of the line, 66779 was the last Class 66 to be built. Specially finished in British Railway lined green, with commemorative outside cab bell, it is named appropriately *Evening Star*. The locomotive has been promised by GBRF to the National Railway Museum on its retirement from service. 9.4.19.

With the success of GBRF's trials of imported gypsum from Hull docks to British Gypsum at Kirkby Thore in September 2002, and with the ten-year 1993 contract with EWS coming to an end, the company took over the workings at Mountfield which started in March 2003. Seen here is the very first working on the branch – 66711 carrying the headboard 'GBRF GYPSUM'. 31.3.03.

GBRF's 100th acquisition, 66734, propels its wagons off the branch. Previously it had seen service in Europe as PB04. The locomotive crossed the Channel from Germany in early 2022. 19.10.22.

The signal on the left of the picture is for site road traffic, not for locomotive drivers. The usual operation would see a constant flashing white light as an indication to drivers to proceed with caution; traffic was called to a halt if a red aspect light was showing. BR Transrail sector-liveried 60085 was eventually sold to Colas Rail and on to GBRF. 9.11.99.

In rainbow livery, inspired by six-year-old Emily Goodman. This unusual livery displayed on 66720 was unveiled in July 2011 at Wansford station on the Nene Valley Railway. 30.9.11.

Prior to demolition of the engine shed the Thomas Hill, Vanguard locos had to be found a new home. British Gypsum No. 1, 183V, was removed to an unknown site in Robertsbridge. It was then sold to Reid Freight Services, Stoke-on-Trent. In 2006 183V was hired to Marcroft Engineering Ltd, Stoke wagon works. In early 2008 Marcroft was sold to DB Schenker, and in 2009 DB started using their own 08 shunters to replace the older industrial types. Unfortunately, in 2009 the loco was sold by Reid's to J. Watson and Sons Ltd, scrap metal merchants, Stafford. 9.11.05.

British Gypsum No. 2, 184V, was also sold to Reid Freight services in 2006 and subsequently hired out to Marcroft in 2008, only to be moved from Marcroft to Electro-Motive Diesel Inc., Longport, in 2009. Its next move came when it was sold by Reid's to Traditional Traction Ltd, Essex, in 2013. From EMD it moved to Locomotion NRM, Shildon, in November 2013 for storage. In March 2014 it was further stored at a site in Warwickshire. In 2016 it was based at The Vale of Berkeley Railway. A need for it at DT Warehouse Ltd, Ely, saw it move there in 2018, only for it to move back to Warwickshire. DB Cargo Maintenance Ltd, Stoke wagon works, hired the locomotive in 2019. Its final move to date was around the end of 2022 when 184V arrived at EG Steel Co. Ltd, Hamilton, Lanarkshire. 9.11.05.

Sporting standard GBRF livery with DMU-style whiskers, 69006, previously 56128, is one of sixteen locomotives converted from former Class 56 traction. The work was carried out by Progress Rail at their workshops in Longport. The wagons are being unloaded by a German-Swiss-manufactured Liebherr A924 wheeled excavator. The offload point remains static whilst the train gradually reverses wagon by wagon down the line.

Named *Peterborough Power Signal Box* in GBRF original livery, 66712 catches the sun beautifully as it starts its trip up the line. 14.3.07.

Almost at the very terminus of the line, EWS 60079 is still in its BR sector main-line livery and named *Foinhaven*. 23.4.01.

The last of the 100-strong Class 60 fleet is seen drawing down the line past the Victorian engine shed. The sunken track of a loop line can clearly be seen. A 1956 map shows this area as 'lorry loading dock' with a covered area with a goods shed too. The trailer astride it belongs to John Jempson and Son, a Rye-based firm. Founded as a horse-drawn timber business in 1866, British Gypsum was the company's principal client for many years. The haulage firm closed in 2024. 28.3.00.

Having arrived from Tonbridge West Yard, the driver has just climbed down from the cab of 69004 to uncouple the locomotive so it can run around the wagons ready for its trip up the branch line. The shunter will then inform the signal box in charge of this section of main line at Robertsbridge of the need to run onto the main line. The signalman would then allow the siding's ground frame to be unlocked, thus permitting travel on to the up line so the running around of the wagons can be achieved. 16.5.22.

Lined up next to Millham Wood, seventeen VTG wagons await the run round of GBRF 66776 *Joanne*. The imported desulphurised powder, gypsum, can clearly be seen piled high in the wagons. 17.6.21.

Just a reminder that although gypsum product arrives at the Mountfield site either by conveyor from the Brightling mine or from the main-line railway, all finished product leaves by road. 16.1.16.

Transrail Freight was formed in 1994 as one of British Rail's trainload freight divisions. 60015 is still in that operator's livery. Owned at this time by EWS, the locomotive is pictured halfway along the branch, its wagons passing behind the engine shed. 13.2.03.

Left: The Victorian engine shed *c*. 1885. Originally built with louvred roof vents, it was unfortunately demolished in 2006.

Below: The engine shed was just about big enough to take two locomotives.

Stopped hard against the footpath to Mountfield Church, 66713 is having its over 1,000-gallon fuel tank replenished by an East Sussex supplier. This practice was only temporary as any spillage would affect the River Line that flows close by and the British Gypsum Fishing Club that has a large lake in the area. 10.5.04.

A picture taken from the top of the southern portal of Mountfield tunnel, GBRF 66739, formerly freightliner 66579, caused disruption to the main line when it derailed on the points whilst running around its wagons. Network Rail staff are using jacking equipment to rerail the loco. 26.4.12.

Above: Proceeding its way through Millham Wood, 66207 heads up the branch with a rare DB Schenker afternoon working from Drax with wagons filled with desulphurised gypsum from the power station. Not becoming a regular working, it was in all probability the first sighting of an EWS/DB-liveried Class 66 in eleven years on the line. 2.3.15.

Left: Powering away from the sidings, 66707 *Sir Sam Fay Great Central Railway* was named at Rushcliffe Halt, Ruddington, in 2003 by his son Edgar Fay QC. 11.6.14.

The pleasant contrasting visual appeal of the line is depicted nicely here as 60003 passes through rolling hills, whilst the wagons slowly trundle behind through Millham Wood heading for the main line. 8.11.02.

66775 is seen through a frame of silver birch trees. It was named *HMS Argyll* at Devonport navy base in July 2017. Before rationalisation of the works' line track, a loop line headed eastward starting from just behind the position of the locomotive. 13.4.18.

Getting the green ground signal to proceed, 66742 *Port of Immingham Centenary 1912-2012* heads on to the main line. In the foreground is a Southern Railway concrete hut manufactured at Exmouth Junction Works. They were designed with the clipped roof to stay within the loading gauge when transported. Designed to accommodate track workers, the interior consisted of a timber bench, table, coat rack and stove. 13.8.16.

Positioned at the foot of the line in dappled lighting, 69005 *Eastleigh*, coupled to 69002, slowly descends the line. 69005, formerly 56007, dominates the scene in its retro Class 33 livery. 8.8.22.

Viewed passing the first of the three level crossings on the line, 66724 displays in early morning sunshine its First Group 'Barbie' livery. In the days of the works railway system a loop line (which in all probability was the original running line) was in situ and ran from a point to the right of the containers, crossing the road, before rejoining the main running line, thus bypassing the first two road crossings. On 8 January 2007 at Old Oak Common the locomotive received its 'Drax Power Station' nameplates. 12.3.15.

Nestled at the end of the sidings, between the Hastings line and the footpath to Eatenden Lane, 66711, with a rake of flat wagons, awaits its next duty. 1.5.04.

Catching the morning light, 66722 *Sir Edward Watkin* powers up the 1 in 40 incline in Metronet branding. Responsible for maintenance, track, signals, etc., Metronet used GBRF locomotives to speed up track replacement works. 13.9.11.

On loan to GBRF, DRS (Direct Rail Services) 66432 makes a fine sight as it hauls a rake of 30-ton containers up the branch for unloading. After running around in the sidings, the trains usually left at 07.20 approximately to go up the branch. 16.5.11.

The first numbered Class 66 in the GBRF fleet, 66701, in the company's original livery design, was delivered to Willesden in March 2001. Unusually, the locomotive is leading down the branch. This would happen sometimes if there was a points failure in the sidings, inhibiting the usual running around of the wagons. 18.1.22.

Mountfield tunnel was one of eight on the Hastings line with reduced dimensions owing to insufficient lining in the tunnels when built by Victorian contractors. The South Eastern Railway subsequently strengthened the tunnels with extra layers of brick which reduced clearances requiring, until 1986, narrower-width locomotives and passenger stock. Running light from Tonbridge West Yard, 66722 runs in to the sidings as a replacement for a failed locomotive on the branch. 14.3.17.

A tipper truck passes 60048 *Eastern* carrying a container from the train to the DSG building's reception bay for unloading. Just out of sight would be the company's Hyster Container Handler that was used for this purpose. 20.1.00.

Still in EWS livery, 66008 rests after some shunting moves in one of the three lines of the exchange sidings – it unusually had finished a nighttime journey up the branch. Acquired from DB Cargo, it went into service with GBRF in December 2017, later to receive, in September 2018, the company's fleet number, 66780. 5.7.18.

Above: Named *Cemex Express* at a ceremony by Pete Waterman at Dove Holes Quarry, Buxton, during 2019, 66780 at the top of the branch was previously with DB Rail and numbered 66008. 4.11.20.

Right: Viewed from a footpath that crosses the line at this location, the route of which winds its way past the exchange sidings and on up over the south portal of Mountfield tunnel. During 2016 when the contract was transferred over to GBRF to run the luxury overnight train from West Coast Railway, 66746 received Belmond Royal Scotsman maroon livery, and entered traffic resplendent with the Great Scottish and Western Railway crest on 18 April 2016. 1.5.13.

In its obsolete Loadhaul livery, EWS 60064 rumbles its way down the branch. The track in the foreground leads to the engine shed. 7.12.99.

A good view of the works site in part can be seen as 60015 *Bow Fell*, set against the giant homogenizer, slowly propels its containers down the branch. 21.3.00.

Framed between a Southern Railway Exmouth Junction-produced lamp post and a redundant works signal, brand-new EWS 66076 works its way past a variety of freshly planted trees up the branch to be unloaded. 9.9.99.

A surviving relic from the past: an incredibly tall (presumably for sighting reasons) out of use signal post which would have protected the entry to the exchange sidings. The fishtail signal arm, later coloured light, would have informed shunter drivers entering the sidings during the railway works era the aspect of the signalling ahead. 3.9.99.

The first four-lever ground frame was in operation until 1956. From then to 1975 a three-lever frame was situated in a hut. The purpose-built cabin shown here was constructed at the time of the Mountfield tunnel singling in 1975. Housing an eleven-lever Stevens Knee Frame, the siding's ground frame has always been a non-block post unable to regulate trains on the main line. 9.6.07.

Pictured in 2017, two interior views of the 1975 signal cabin. The ground frame has always come under the control of Robertsbridge box, the signalman there giving the release to Mountfield ground frame to let trains be signalled in and out of the sidings.

Arriving trains are halted at a signal on the down line north of Mountfield tunnel. The ground frame operator would then be able to clear a subsidiary signal to pass the main aspect there so trains could run into the sidings on exiting the tunnel.

Still carrying BR sector Railfreight Metals and Automotive branding, EWS-owned 60031 passes a 1986 Hastings electrification substation as it heads up the branch. 11.4.02.

The first of its class, 69001 *Mayflower*, named after the ship that carried the pilgrims from Plymouth to the New World, represents the link between GBRF and Progress Rail, an American company with workshops in Longport, England, where the class are converted from redundant Class 56 locomotives. 18.1.22.

A crossing gate worker takes a break as 66714 *Cromer Lifeboat* passes over the first of three crossings on the branch. These containers were ordered by British Gypsum from Transtech OY in Finland. Forty-eight boxes were delivered to the company in November 1993 and a further forty-eight in early spring 1994. 26.4.13.

A view looking past 60081 *Isambard Kingdom Brunel* toward the very top of the branch, the roadway to the right goes to the reception area where the gypsum containers are taken from the train for unloading. 15.2.03.

Due to a landslip closing the line at High Brooms near Tunbridge Wells on the Hastings line, Mountfield trains were required to reverse at Robertsbridge. This necessitated the train having locomotives at both ends of the wagons. Here 66771 *Amanda* with 59003 out of sight makes for an unusual event, as locomotives leading down the branch are quite rare. 11.2.21.

A chance to view 59003 *Yeoman Highlander* on the tail end. After reversal at Robertsbridge the train regained its scheduled route via Hastings, Ashford and Tonbridge. 9.2.21.

In a Christmas card setting, 66715 and wagons are being propelled down once again by 59003. The reversal at Robertsbridge will be carried out by using the crossover just north of the station 8.2.21.

Mountfield exchange sidings had a surprise visitor in the shape of Class 73 Electro Diesel 73212 arriving at the line to shunt some container wagons. 11.7.11.

Having worked up the branch to use the company's container handler, 73212 returns down the line. The locomotive is in de-branded First Group livery. 11.7.11.

Forty minutes were spent at the top of the branch on the container move before 73212 returned to the exchange sidings. The driver and shunter chat over the next shunting moves. 11.7.11.

EWS 60095 subsequently to this date spent four years with Colas Rail before eventually being acquired by GBRF. 22.5.01.

With the introduction in 1998 of EWS Class 66s into the country, 66050 is just one of the class that started to dominate freight services. The Mountfield workings was no exception, with the inevitable reduction in Class 60 workings. 30.6.99.

On occasions locomotives that might otherwise be left in the sidings overnight would be, for security reasons, brought up onto the branch and stabled at various places. At one time the area to the right of the picture was the site of a loop line later reduced to a short siding. 5.4.03.

Nearly fifteen years have passed and now 66714 is stabled next to the lorry wheel wash where once the engine shed stood. The roadway leads up into the main works. On the extreme left is the lorry weighbridge. 12.11.17.

Class 33s operated Mountfield services for many years, 33202 makes for an astonishing sight on its old stomping ground to perform a wagon shunting move. The loco is on loan from its owners FM Rail to GBRF. Originally designated D6587, it was eventually sold into preservation in 2009. Assisting with this surprise working are two Class 73 locos, 73206 and 73206. 16.2.05.

The Mountfield Line Since 2000

Unusually double-headed, 66714 *Cromer Lifeboat* leads 66702 *Blue Lightning*. The reason for the extra motive power is not because of an engine failure, rather it's because of operating reasons in the Southampton area. 11.5.04.

Three days of disruption ensued when Freightliner locomotive 66564 came off the track whilst leaving the sidings for the main line. Network Rail staff are seen in the process of jacking the wheels of the locomotive back onto the line. 29.4.25.

To the rescue! 66567 runs in wrong road from the tunnel. Once in the sidings it will pull the wagons clear from derailed locomotive 66564. 29.4.25.

The clapboard building stood on ground adjacent to the extensive gardens of Little Millham, the original mine manager's house, and is thought to be the second weighbridge office. The original, situated slightly to the east, was operated for years by a Mr Crouch who lived in a cottage converted from the Mill Rooms by the railway boundary gate. 60050 eventually went into preservation at the Wensleydale Railway. 9.2.00.

GBRF locomotive 66703, named *Doncaster PSB 1981-2002*, celebrating twenty-one years of the power signal box. 7.4.17.

In the days when the works shunters plied their wagons between the mine area and the exchange sidings, catchpoints were commonplace due to the falling gradient of the line. This section in the foreground by 66716, now the car park, was laid an escape track designed to halt any runaway wagons. 1.7.04.

With a nice view up the branch, 66747 hauls its JNA wagons for unloading. Introduced into Mountfield Gypsum trains in November 2018, replacing the 1993 containers. 8.4.21.

It was standard practice at the time to bring down a crossing barrier on the north side of the first crossing. The south side was devoid of one, so a company vehicle was used as a block to traffic. EWS 60070 *John Loudon McAdam* in Loadhaul livery makes its way to the sidings. 30.9.02.

Still in Colas livery but in fact a GBRF locomotive with their numbering, 66744 slowly draws forward its empty wagons onto the Hastings line. 26.1.12.

In Metronet livery 66720 *Metronet Pathfinder* in perfect sunshine backs down into the sidings. 5.6.07.

Celebrity-liveried Class 60 No. 081 at the halfway point down the branch, delivered November 1991 in Trainload Metals sector branding and named *Bleaklow Hill*, later gained this new-lined GWR Brunswick green livery and was renamed *Isambard Kingdom Brunel*. 15.2.03.

With its distinctive rectangular buffers and extended horn box, 66794 in Railfreight triple grey livery drops down the branch. Its first use was in Europe at ERS Netherlands, then at Heavy Haul Power in Germany. In 2020 it arrived in the UK to expand the GBRF fleet. 7.12.21.

Switched off at the end of the exchange sidings, 08847 was hired in from Cotswold Rail for a short period by GBRF to split and shunt the containers on overlong trains. 28.5.03.

A few runs were made over the lower part of the branch, however the 08 had a very short life at Mountfield, eventually going to PD Ports, Grangetown, Middlesbrough. 27.5.03.

In honour of Harry Beck who created the London Underground Tube map of 1933, 66721 carries a detailed print of the network within its livery. 22.9.17.

The office windows of the Gypsum company have a splendid view of operations at the top of the branch. EWS 66159 later would work in Poland for DB Schenker Polska. Built in 1999, the locomotive was less than a year old in this view. 27.1.00.

Acquired from Direct Rail Services in 2011 passing down the branch, 66416 is seen in Freightliner PowerHaul livery. 6.5.25.

After a minor derailment of the branch, some track laying took place. So, Balfour Beatty Rail brought to the line their USA Canron Tamper Vibratool to tamper the ballast after track relaying. 14.10.04.

A walker on the footpath between Netherfield's Victorian church and All Saints in Mountfield would have no doubt enjoyed the interlude from their stroll to observe this main-line locomotive crossing their path in such a tranquil spot. Brand-new 69008 *Richard Howe*, named after Network Rail's controller, was engineered using the body shell of a Class 56, in this case 56038. 11.10.23.

Carrying the title *The Flying Dustbin*, as named by Biffa's own staff, 66783's distinctive livery adds some cheeriness to a dull day. 22.12.22.

The Mountfield Line Since 2000

There was much excitement at Toton open day during August 1998 when 66005 was put on display as one of only four of the class in the country at the time. In a hi-vis-free era, driver and shunter work together to bring the train down the line. 26.8.99.

Large BR logo 66789, previously EWS's last purchased loco 66250. The driver is equipped with two-way radio for the reversing moves and keeps in communication with the shunter who, with a combination of walking and staff van to drive ahead of the wagons, talks the train back to the sidings. 16.12.20.

Lorries all around, yet the eye is drawn to retro BR Research-liveried 69004 basking in the summer sunshine, resting up between the first and second road crossings. Between workings light locomotives tend to be stabled up the branch away from the main line. 18.8.22.

Due to weekend engineering works 66752 *The Hoosier State*, referencing Indiana, USA, where the loco was built, leads down the line top and tailing with out of sight 66777. The train was pathed to operate along the Medway Valley line through Maidstone away from its usual Sevenoaks route, necessitating the second locomotive for the train's reversal at Tonbridge. 3.2.18.

The brake van when attached to the last wagon of the train is a 'Propelling Control Vehicle' fitted with an emergency brake valve to be controlled by the shunter if required in an emergency when talking the train back using two-way radios with the driver. The vehicle is in faded Loadhaul livery, is situated at the end of the exchange sidings and was out of use when the photograph was taken. 10.12.02.

Unloading always started at the end of the train. 60099 *Ben More Assynt*, with one last container to collect, will soon start its journey back down the line. 15.12.00.

Mountfield Trains on the Hastings Line and Other Lines

The 25-mile section of the Hastings Line between Tunbridge Wells and St Leonards passes mostly through rural countryside. Passing a foreground of meadow buttercups heading towards Wadhurst, 69005 has come to the rescue of failed 69004. In the late spring sunshine the pair make for a colourful sight. 17.5.22.

In almost perfect BR Loadhaul livery 60007 has just left Mountfield tunnel. 17.3.03.

The Mountfield Line Since 2000

The rolling fields of Etchingham looking towards Hurst Green. EWS 66159 approaches Etchingham station. 27.1.99.

Etchingham station opened in 1851. 69001, formerly 56031, in full sun, charges through the station on its way to Southampton. 22.6.22.

6 miles up the Hastings line from Mountfield, 66718 *Peter Lord Hendy of Richmond Hill*, sporting a special London 150th anniversary livery, passes through Etchingham. A map of the station from 1873 shows a wagon turntable situated to the right of the locomotive that fed a track crossing the running lines at right angles. 1.3.24.

A view of 69008 from Tonbridge station bridge. 24.8.24.

Wadhurst is an important commuter station around 1 mile from the village at the foot of a steep hill. 66502 *Basford Hall Centenary 2001* proceeds towards Tonbridge. 12.2.25.

Heavy freight locomotive 60003 travels between Mountfield and Robertsbridge. Named *Freight Transport Association*, that company eventually became Logistics UK, based in Tunbridge Wells, six stations up the line. 29.1.03.

The last Class 66 to be built passes delightful surroundings north of Etchingham. Its appearance is based on BR Class 9F 92220 *Evening Star*, which was the last steam locomotive built by British Railways, and is itself named *Evening Star*. 20.4.19.

Named *Maritime One* in September 2016, 66727 and wagons pass Robertsbridge signal box. This is the box that releases the Mountfield ground frame allowing trains access in and out of Mountfield sidings. 1.3.23.

Waiting in the old Kent and East Sussex Railways Bay platform at Robertsbridge, 66720 has travelled light engine from Mountfield sidings for refuelling. This procedure was never an ideal situation and didn't last for long with the processes soon to be regularly performed at St Leonards Depot. 6.6.07.

Tonbridge West Yard has always played an important role in service to the Mountfield workings, stabling locomotives and wagons over many years. 69002 *Bob Tiller CM&EE*, rebuilt from 56311, enters the yard from Mountfield. The usual pattern was for trains to travel from Mountfield midday to Southampton direct, loaded trains returning overnight with a layover at Tonbridge West Yard before departure to Mountfield sidings during the early hours. 14.9.22.

Previously a fast line freight locomotive then passing to DRS, eventually acquired in August 2022 by GBRF, the loco still retains its DRS Blue livery. 66302 passes Etchingham on the long 1 in 50 climb to Wadhurst. 22.8.24.

On the horizon above the trees, the spire of St Stephen's Church stands tall over Tonbridge as 60018 takes the curve toward Hildenborough. This locomotive and another, 60017, were the first two of the class to be accepted into traffic in October 1990. 20.2.02.

The Mountfield Line Since 2000

Approaching Mountfield tunnel, FM Rail 33202 *Meteor* with 73209 and 73206 are on a wagon-shunting move to Mountfield from Tonbridge West Yard. The 73s were added for train-formation reasons. 16.2.05.

Arriving from Sweden in 2019 to boost the GBRF fleet, 66791 passes Robertsbridge signal box, painted in Southern Railway period green and cream colours. The box is the only surviving one left on the Hastings line. It controls the line from north of Battle to north of Stonegate. 28.9.23.

Tonbridge West Yard. After twenty-five years of GBRF operating the Mountfield Gypsum trains, the contact went to Freightliner. Awaiting the company's debut on the service, 66508 waits to haul its first train to Mountfield. 5.10.24.

Just north of Mountfield tunnel 60081 *Isambard Kingdom Brunel* was named on 5 August 2000 at Old Oak Common. In March 2024 the locomotive went to Margate's The One, for static display. 14.2.03.

Named as the best place in England to live by the *Sunday Times*, Wadhurst lies on a high wooded ridge in the Weald. Passing a row of country cottages in Station Road, 69003 is the third of the class to enter traffic and formerly was 56018. The first locomotives were essentially based at Tonbridge, and early testing was carried out on the Mountfield trains. 13.4.22.

In MSC livery 66709 rushes through Etchingham station, which is Grade II listed and is built on the site of Etchingham Manor. Previously in GBRF/Medite shipping livery, 66709 in 2012 was rebranded featuring a large container ship image and named *Sorrento*. 26.7.22.

Exiting the north portal of Mountfield tunnel 66734 double heads with 69001. During 2022 it received its nameplate, *Platinum Jubilee*. 19.10.22.

At Grosvenor Road bridge 66794 *Steve Hannam* heads for Southampton. In retro trainload petroleum sector markings, it is passing the site of what was once Tunbridge Wells Central Goods. 30.11.21.

Etchingham 66780 *The Cemex Express*. The Hastings line, unlike so many others in the South East, still enjoys this regular freight working. 15.10.20.

60015 *Bow Fell* in Transrail livery is seen having just exited Mountfield tunnel. 13.2.03.

An unidentified Class 60 in Railfreight Metals sector livery passes over the River Rother near Robertsbridge. 4.4.02.

On a down working from Tonbridge West Yard 66796 *The Green Progressor* passes through Robertsbridge. The bay platform was once used by trains to Tenterden and Headcorn and is now a siding leading to the Rother Valley Railway. 4.5.23.

Approaching the Tonbridge to Ashford main line, 66710 emerges from Somerhill tunnel. The line through the tunnel was singled on electrification in 1986 which brought an end to the use of special width stock which had always been needed due the narrow tunnels on the line. 23.1.05.

De-branded Freightliner locomotive still carrying its predecessor's number, 66581, heads north towards Wadhurst. Cascaded across to GBRF, the loco became 66741.

GBRF celebrates Queen Elizabeth II's Golden Jubilee with appropriate Union Jack flag and nameplate adoring the locomotive. Swinging off the Hastings line, 66705 joins the route from Ashford. 27.6.11.

Imported from Germany in 2021, 66797 in Beacon Rail livery passes Robertsbridge. The wagons are passing the former site of John Stenning and Son's sawmill which on old maps shows a connecting siding and a narrow-gauge works railway system. It closed in 1986. 31.1.24.

Farewell to the container wagons after nearly twenty-five years of service, 66781 on a special Saturday working hauls its load to Middlesbrough Dawson GBRF for a new contract of traffic to Hotchley Hill on the GCR. The train has just passed Etchingham. 4.11.18.

Viewed from what once would have been the Tonbridge goods lines, 66793 rounds the curve at the top of the Hastings line, carrying heritage BR construction livery. It was frequently referred to as a Euro Class 66, as the locomotive operated in Germany until 2021. 14.9.21.

On Friday 28 March 2003 EWS got their last ever train away from Mountfield and they did it in style. Heavy freight 60033 *Tees Steel Express* in 'Corus' livery rumbles away from Mountfield tunnel and off into Hastings line history. 28.3.03.

Aggregate Industries, based at Bardon Hill, Coalville, and GBRF have a contract together that's run since 2014. The loco was named on 2 July 2015 after the River Sence and the project to re-route the river around their Bardon Hill site. 66711 *Sence* is seen approaching Robertsbridge. 12.3.21.

Passing a typical English byway 66767, in GBRF semicircle livery, is spotted running by Bishops Lane in a rural setting near Robertsbridge. 13.8.20.

Freightliner took over the Gypsum train workings to Southampton in October 2024. 66539 passes Etchingham during the first week of operations. 9.10.24.

In bright sunshine between Etchingham and Wadhurst, 60039 looks very smart in its new EWS livery. Formerly the locomotive was in Railfreight Construction identity and was named *Glastonbury Tor*. 1.3.02.

Frant station is a Grade II listed building and looks out over gloriously undeveloped countryside. 69005 is actually passing Bells Yew Green, which is a mile from Frant Village itself, on its way to Southampton. 19.12.23.

Mountfield tunnel was the first to collapse in 1855 because of insufficient tunnel lining. This was rectified by possibly utilising a brick field again that was in operation near the tunnel when the line was built. Named *Mam Tor*, 60082's containers are still emerging from the tunnel.15.4.02.

Robertsbridge signal box. The extension to the signal box was built to house the extra equipment when the line was electrified in 1986. On railway land behind the box once stood Mr Chandler's 'Station Garage' for new cars and repairs, dispenser of petrol and paraffin. 6.1.25.

Of all of the Class 66 special liveries 66789 *British Rail 1948-1997* in BR blue with large logo arguably catches the eye of the enthusiast the most. The locomotive passes through open countryside toward Wadhurst. 16.12.20.

It is so rare to see Mountfield trains travelling south of its sidings. 66729 *Derby County* in LNER-inspired football crests is seen at Crowhurst, former junction for the Bexhill West Branch, and is being routed to Tonbridge via Hastings and Ashford. 66722 is bringing up the rear. 3.2.21.

Wascosa-liveried 66720 is about to plunge into Mountfield tunnel having just left the sidings. Previously in GBRF rainbow livery, the company formed a partnership with the company to supply wagons for UK Rail Infrastructure Services. 19.12.22.

Traversing the curve under a farm occupation bridge into Stonegate station is 66706 *Nene Valley*. The locomotive was named at the preserved Nene Valley Railway in April 2003.

Near Wadhurst, Sussex, this farming county is on display to full effect as 66713 travels through delightful pastureland. The line runs parallel to the River Rother at this point which flows behind the trees. 9.1.19.

Approaching Church Lane bridge, Etchingham, 69004 in retro BR 'Rail Research' livery has come to the rescue of failed 69003. The striking livery symbolises GBRF's and Network Rail's operations at Rail Innovation and Development Centre's high-speed test track at Melton Mowbray in Leicestershire. 5.2.23.

A mid-afternoon working from Drax Power Station, 66716 double-heads with 66713. Extra power was provided due to the re-routing of the train over steeply graded lines around the London area. 14.5.04.

On the last day of March 2003 GBRF 66711 hauls the company's first train to Southampton, a working the company will operate for the next twenty years. The no-fuss nameplate reads *GBRF GYPSUM*. 31.3.03.

Set in the High Weald, Stonegate station is surrounded almost totally by Sussex countryside, typifying the atmosphere of the Hastings line. 60031, formally named *Ben Lui*, passes through its deserted platforms. 8.4.02.

Near Etchingham, 66747 *Made in Sheffield* NWT is a Sheffield haulage company; GBRF runs its containers to their Rotherham terminal. 14.4.21.

Used by Rudyard Kipling during the 1920s and '30s, Robertsbridge station is the junction station for the Rother Valley Railway. 60079 *Foinaven* passes through. 23.4.01.

Near Winchester, the Mountfield to Southampton working passes Shawford. 66748 was built for Belgian operator Crossrail Benelux. It was purchased by GBRF in 2012, and during 2015 the loco was painted into GBRF's blue and orange livery. 25.6.15.

Nearing journey's end at Southampton, 60097 *Foinaven* passes through Eastleigh. The Southampton import traffic started in late 1998, making it an either/or supply with Drax Power Station. 26.4.01.

At Upper Holloway on the Gospel Oak to Barking line, 66708 is on a Mountfield to Doncaster working. 27.4.10.

Diverted 66752 on the Mountfield to Southampton train at Wateringbury on the Medway Valley Railway line. The train had been top and tailed with 66777 on its return run between Tonbridge Yard and Mountfield. The second locomotive was removed with the train's reversal at Tonbridge. 3.2.18.

Approaching Winchelsea on The Marsh line between Hastings and Ashford, 59003 hauls a diverted Mountfield to Southampton train. During this period it was in all probability the only time a Class 59 worked the Mountfield trains. 12.2.21.

Railtours to Mountfield

The Diamond Twenties railtour celebrating sixty years of the Class 20 locomotives. GBRF 20205 and 20189 with 73963 and 73141 at the rear runs into the sidings from London Victoria. The two pairs of locomotives swapped ends in the sidings for the run up the branch. 5.5.18.

Emerging from the Millham Wood, 73141 and 73963 return back down the branch to the sidings. 5.5.18.

Passing the boundary gate, the chocolate and cream coaches of the train pass through into the sidings. The driver of 20189 and 20205 takes in the historic scene. 5.5.18.

The Diamond Twenties railtour travelled from Mountfield to Tonbridge and onward to Ashford to reach the Romney Marsh and the Dungeness branch in Kent. Passing Dungeness water tower, 73141 and 73963 are nearing the end of the line. 5.5.18.

Closed to passengers in 1967, the freight-only Dungeness branch hosts the Diamond Twenties railtour. 20205 and 20189 pass the former Brookland station on its way back to London Victoria via Maidstone East. 5.5.18.

Entering the sidings at Mountfield, 73208 tails 73141 on The Mine of Serpents railtour from Waterloo. 5.11.11.

Making its way on a dull autumn day, 73208 *Kirsten* leads The Mine of Serpents railtour away from the sidings. The tour was named after a firework of the same name, and as the tour was visiting a mine and it ran on 5 November, it seemed appropriate. 5.11.11.

The Mine of Serpents railtour halfway up the branch. 73208 was one of five classmates that were put through a rebuilding programme, becoming 73965. It is crossing the original roadway that gave access to the site from Mountfield's Church Lane. The science company shown on the direction board was located at Milham. The second house, built for the manager of the mine, in turn became their main office before being sold to Photonic. 5.11.11.

The return journey down the branch of The Mine of Serpents railtour with 73141 in ex-GBRF 'First' livery leading. From Mountfield the tour ran through to the Bluebell Railway via London Bridge then back to Waterloo, which was the tour's starting point. 5.11.11.

Passing Special Workings

Steaming nicely past the exchange sidings in glorious afternoon sunshine, LMS Stanier Class 44871 powers a London Victoria–Eastbourne–Hastings–London Victoria 'Steam Dreams' excursion. The trackside greenery and the single wagon at the end of the siding add to the scene. 22.6.19.

Eatenden Road level crossing. 57310 in Network Rail livery crawls wrong road through an engineer's possession, destination Hoo Junction. Also known as Riverhill crossing, Mountfield, its roughly situated adjacent to the end of the exchange sidings. 7.12.13.

Traveling light loco 66733 is making its way to St Leonards Depot from Hoo Junction for maintenance. 66751 waits in the siding for the single track through the tunnel to clear before it can depart. 20.1.17.

Opening for business in 1909, Balfour Beatty are a worldwide construction and infrastructure company that includes rail. 1960s-built Class 20s Nos 901 and 905 travel light loco on an Ashford–Victoria–East Kent driver training trip. 11.8.25.

Locomotive Services day five of a six-day tour from Canterbury to Crewe. 37688 *Great Rocks* in 'Railfreight Construction' identity leads D6851 *Flopsie* in BR Brunswick green livery between Eatenden Lane crossing and the sidings. 18.4.22.

A VSOE British Pullman luxury train day excursion to Rye and Battle is about to plunge into the gloom of Mountfield tunnel. Immaculate-looking 47792 *Robin Hood* passes the sidings. 11.7.03.

The birth of modern railways was honoured in 2025. One of many events that took place that year, celebrated as 'Railway 200', was in Ashford Kent. Returning from the event, 73128 *Kent and East Sussex Railway* (named to mark that railway's 50th anniversary in 2024) hauls a rake of Hastings Diesels Ltd stock back to its home at St Leonards Works. 25.8.25.

Sadly, with less than a year of operation ahead of it Network Rail De-icer and Sandite unit 930006, originally formed in 1979 from the driving coaches of Ex-Sub 4380, takes the curve through a still-leafy Hastings line. Any leaf mulch problems on the gypsum line are resolved by a man walking up the line dispensing sand from a watering can. 3.11.03.

As part of the 'Seaford Line 150' celebrations BR Standard Class 7 70013 *Oliver Cromwell* passed the branch working a London Victoria–Seaford–Hastings–Victoria excursion. 7.6.14.

The Network Rail test train hauled by 73138 awaits a green signal before entering into Mountfield tunnel on its journey to Selhurst from Three Bridges. 18.5.11.

A Hoo Junction to Robertsbridge engineer's train hauled by Colas Rail 70807 passes slowly through the possession near Eatenden Lane crossing. 15.11.14.

Contracted to haul the Network Test train, Colas Rail's ex-preservation loco 37025 *Inverness TMD* is seen on a cold January afternoon heading for Woking from Hither Green. 21.7.17.

The Class 67 locomotives were mainly procured by EWS for the travelling post office trains. After Royal Mail decided the transportation of mail by rail would end in 2004 one of the new uses for the class was on the prestigious VSOE workings. 67023 is hauling empty coaching stock to Hither Green having worked an excursion to Rye and Battle. 15.5.04.

The architecturally interesting Methodist Chapel in Eatenden Lane built in 1894 had seen 125 years of trains by the time that 66714 leading 66704 went by on a Tonbridge West Yard rail head treatment train. 24.1.19.

Against the backdrop of Lots Wood, Battle of Britain Class 34067 *Tangmere* makes for an impressive sight as it charges its way up the line on 'The Romney Marsh Lunchtime tour'. 21.6.11.

A busy scene as four GBRF Class 73 locomotives head for St Leonards Works from Tonbridge West Yard. 69005 will depart the siding as soon as the convoy clears the single line section. 8.8.22.

On a Dollands Moor to Woking test train Colas Rail Freight 37219 crosses Eatenden Lane. Behind the locomotive once stood a two-storey crossing-keeper's cottage. The small ivy-strewn replacement has seen better days. 1.10.16.

Class 47 locomotives were introduced throughout the 1960s. Between 1998 and 2004 over thirty were re-engined and became Class 57. Approaching Eatenden Lane crossing, GBRF 57310, formerly 47831, is on a circular journey from Tonbridge via Rye. 11.8.25.

The driver of 73212 has a good view of the sidings in this wintery picture as a snow and ice treatment train hastens by on a working to Ashford. In the distance next to the signal cabin can be seen the target symbol on the access gate to the start of the branch. 11.2.21.

'The Channel Coast Express' excursion hauled by West Coast Railway's 47804 is twenty minutes into its five-hour return journey back to Barnetby from Hastings. It was then and still is a good spot to watch trains go by. 25.4.11.

The Brightling Mine

The Brightling. The conveyor was installed in 1989, replacing an aerial ropeway system. The mine now transports cement rock for the cement industry.

The Mountfield Line Since 2000

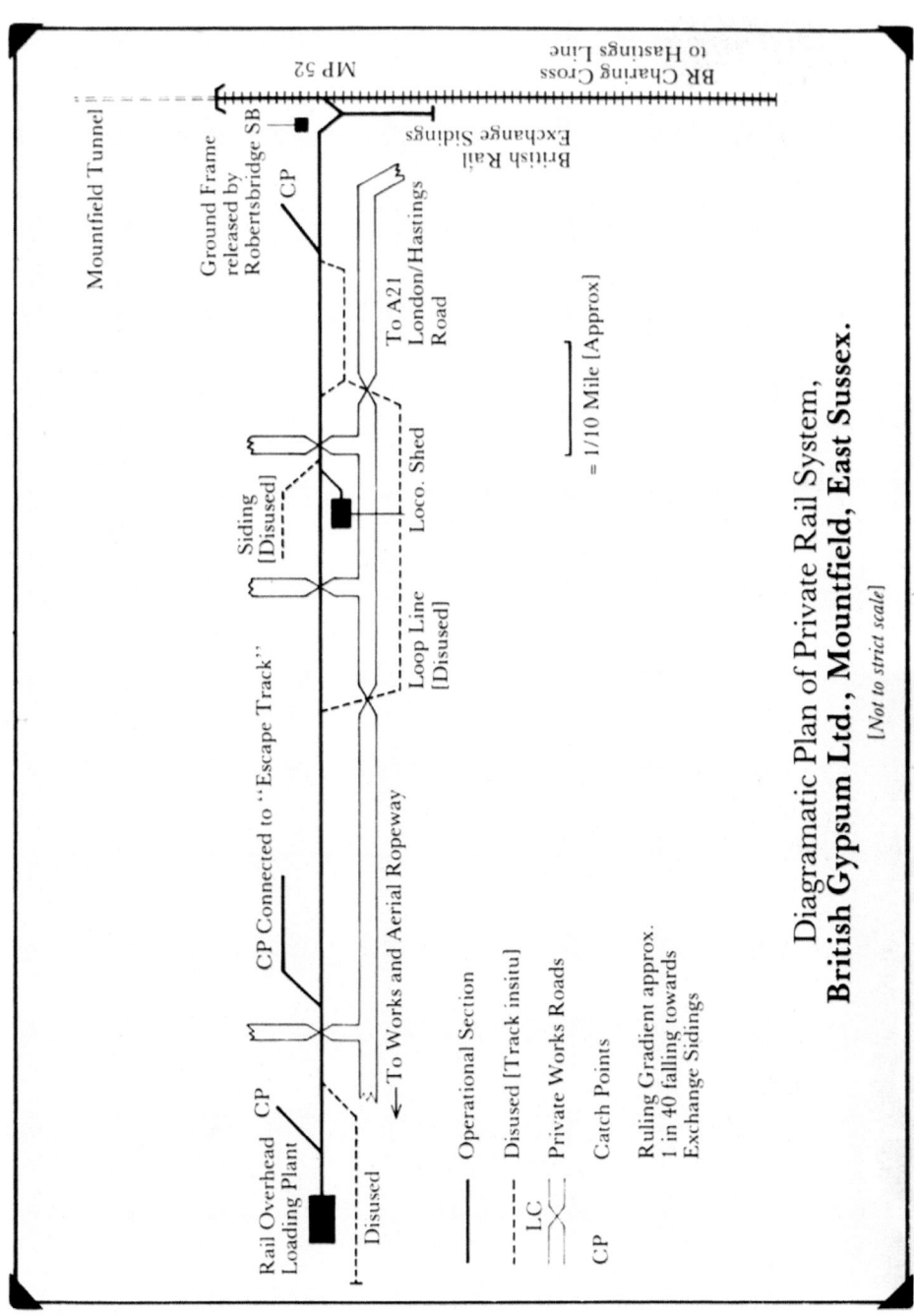

Diagrammatic plan of the private rail system.

Bibliography and Acknowledgements

Dalston, H., 'The Mountfield Gypsum Mine Tramway', *The Railway Magazine* (February 1950)
Industrial Railway Society, *Industrial Railways and Locomotives of Surrey and Sussex*
Johnson, Norman, 'The Mountfield Gypsum Line', *Tenterden Terrier*, No. 36
Jones, Trish, *Mountfield Meanderings* (books 1 and 2; Mountfield Village Hall local history archive)
The Sussex Industrial Archaeology Society, No. 14 (1984)

British Gypsum Mountfield: A Change in Direction, the films of Keven Burchett (YouTube)
Six Bells Junction rail tour information website

I would like to thank the following people for their contributions and help in compiling this book: Adrian Nicholls, Trish Jones, Alison Beaven, Tony Hagon, Stuart Searle, Tim Saunders, John Hunt, David Alderton of the Battle and District Historical Society and Network Rail.

All photographs at Mountfield where either taken from footpaths or with permission from works staff on site at the time. All photographs are by the author unless otherwise stated.